The Miseducation of the Negro in the 21st Century

by

Cedric A. Washington

The MISEDUCATION of the Negro in the 21st Century

© 2025 by Cedric A. Washington

All rights reserved.

For permission requests, write to the publisher at the address below.

Who Lives Like This?! Publishing LLC

www.nerdyouthservices.org

ISBNs:

Hardcover: 978-1-970680-01-0

Paperback: 978-1-970680-04-01

Digital (Online): 978-1-970680-07-2

Cover design and interior layout by Who Lives Like This?! Publishing LLC Design Team

Printed in the United States of America

First Edition — 2025

06/25/2010

I dedicate...

Born four months apart, middle school, high school, and first semester of college, we literally grew up together. The countless stories, the partying, the laughs, the music, the stepping (we always danced), we weren't siblings, but it sure felt like it. Energy cannot be created nor destroyed. And, with that being said the spirit never dies. I dedicate this important piece of work to my family. Special shout out to my cousin, Candace Marie Smith. 11/30/77-07/18/22. Love is love. Peace.

The Miseducation of the Negro in the 21st Century

Cedric A. Washington

Foreword

This is a compilation of speeches written through subject matter chaptered, living, researching, and speaking on the experiences of the miseducation of the Negro in the 21st Century. As the awakening of the intelligence of the so-called African Americans begins to gain their conscience collectively across the world, those that are tasked with the charge to unite our people must share their knowledge and teach their truth. The Miseducation of the Negro in the 21st Century is a message to the white liberals that teach in urban education, the black figurehead principals and leaders that perpetuate the systemic nuances of standard education in America, the people living in the inner cities across the nation that share the sentiments of a flawed system, hip-hop, politics, and the black church.

The so-called 'African American' community will never catapult to the level they should be if white people control mainstream education. The condition of education in the black community is past a reset. It needs to be scrapped and revamped. The objective is to give an insight no different than hip-hop did mainstream America when it introduced itself to the world, widening the lenses of the public to an up close and personal perspective we know as, rap music. This is a synopsis through the eyes of someone in the culture of urban education; That is black. Grew up, black. Educated, black. Work, black. Live, black. The miseducation of the negro in the 21st Century.

Preface

The academic system known as education can stifle the pedagogy of the best teachers because you must teach in the ramifications of state standards. Mainstream text and curriculums alike are pushed through urban education and there is not a teacher or administrator I know that does not have complaints about the lack of cultural competency most mainstream text and curriculum provides. Yet, we must turn water into wine, lemons to lemonade, and make the best out of what we have and that's why urban education is equivalent to Soul Food. Despite the scraps, lack of resources, undervalued feelings, and overall unhealthiness of the situation, black educators still make what we do look good! *Give yourselves a round of applause*

I am a free man. I was institutionalized in the constraints of traditional education. Although I was the Malcolm X of education in my approach with teaching it only provided me with a grand opening, grand closing ceremony every year, I kept getting fired. I could never find myself compliant with the rules and regulations of the system and how they wanted us to interact with our students versus how I knew to naturally be with our students. I have worked in academic institutions where a demerit/merit system was in play. All actions were data driven. If a student broke a rule, the objective was to reprimand the student and document the student's action and comment on the method of discipline I used. We were tracking behavioral data. My problem was I would redirect a student and keep moving. "Tuck your shirt in. Okay, Mr. Washington.," and that was it. The student tucks in their shirt and we both continue our day. So, when it was time for my observations and check-ins with my overseer, Instructional Lead, Dean of Instruction, Academic Coach whatever the title is, I lacked the proper data, and it came off like I am insubordinate or "bucking the system." Ultimately, I was interacting normally. Redirect, student correct behavior, keep it moving. What I could do naturally, I was wrongly judged because I did not follow the rules of the school, as to how they treat discipline. That is when I understood that schools pride themselves on a model versus listening to the expert, me.

I could not help but think about my personal school experience, elementary, middle school, and high school. I thought about college and the classes I took to be prepared for my career. And, I thought, if I am in front of these students that look like me, and I know how I was taught and what worked for me, why wouldn't I teach the way I was taught if it benefited me to the degree that I am the person in front of students teaching. That was my crash course of learning how these pop-up shop schools work. White people produce models and theories based on research that they think can benefit our people. Then we (black people) perpetuate the system by buying into something that we figure out isn't working because we have BILLS. That is when what is a passion for some or even a deliberate career choice for others becomes HELL. We must put an end to people coming into our communities proclaiming themselves to be the expert on what is best for us. It is hurting us, and no one is brave enough to admit it because we are in a position where we must maintain households.

So, we turn water into Hennessey. Something that is bad for us and ruins your body down the line if you do not change. We put out products that we know are not real. We graduate kids that are not academically

Cedric A. Washington

prepared to go to any next level of learning. We are perpetuating a crime that these pop-up shop institutions are doing in our communities to our "babies," as we like to say. It is time to get courageous and become free. Become free of the shackles of intellectual jargon about things that does not make sense, become free of teaching our students state standards of empty rhetoric that does not reflect the imagery of our kids, interest our students or teachers then expect our students to perform miracles because they're not properly prepared to pass any test that's OPENLY biased. We have schools that do not have libraries, gyms, computer labs and yet we talk about preparing students to be college ready. It is a crime! The time is now for true change. The time is now to take over our education, take over discipline, take over our culture and communities because we have allowed the powers that be to dictate what we do and how we do to the point where the kids have spun out of control and lost their minds.

I am a free man. My purpose and objective are to save my people, teach my people, empower my people. Knowledge of S.E.L.F. Curriculum does just that. My professional developments for teachers do just that. My workshops for the youth do just that. The last shall be first, and the first shall be last; that time is here now. It is time for us to be bold. Be brave. The time is now to take over and control our destiny. Education is a systemic way to instruct a group of people or person on what to learn. Knowledge is information and experience that prepares you to have intelligence to learn from and teach others. Can you be educated and still be clueless? That is called slavery. If you are controlled to do something that goes against your internal thought as to what is best, that's slavery. If you can admit to yourselves that education has, and it is getting progressively worse on every front imaginable then it is time to take a different approach. It is time to start using the sense that is not so common. It is time to begin to understand that for people to cultivate their culture they must control their culture. N.E.R.D. (Nurturing Education Rewarding Determination) Youth Services, Inc. is an organization designed to empower the so-called African American youth. Project UPLIFT Mentoring program caters to both boys and girls, young men, and women alike to be empowered through one-to-one mentoring and group mentoring. Using the curriculum Knowledge of S.E.L.F (Social Empowerment Learning Framework) topics and activities are facilitated for our people so that they can relate to and be provided with the necessary insight to become better people. My people, the time is now. I need your help. I need your support. Help me help the community, promote greatness, and have every institution in America be impacted culturally by their own. A cat cannot teach a duck how to swim. When we know better, we should begin to do better. It is so.

Cedric A. Washington

THE MISEDUCATION OF THE NEGRO
IN THE 21ST CENTURY

Chapter 1

Privilege.

There has been a deficit of learning in black America surrounding education dating back to the 1980s; Every decade. Since the mid-nineties and skyrocketing through the 2000s, pop up shop institutions known as charter schools have dominated the educational sector in urban America. Public school systems are slowly diminishing to non-existent while white businessmen and women alike conform ideologies to create a plan to bridge the gap of the academic disproportionality that is a plague in various inner cities throughout the United States. In fact, public school vs. charter school is now an age-old debate surrounding the qualifications of who is best suited to teach the African American youth. Charter schools are frowned upon by some in the educational industry for their lenient policies regarding certification status for teachers, non-traditional grading scales which may benefit the student to have a better chance to pass a class versus the traditional public school system, to even the influx of white teachers educating black students, in black schools, in black neighborhoods. And, with all the educational rhetoric and intellectual banter, we still forget the words of Dr. Carter G. Woodson when he wrote on how we drifted away from the truth in which is a chapter in the book, 'The Mis-Education of the Negro.'

Woodson explained, "The people who maintained schools for the education of certain Negroes before the Civil War were certainly sincere; and so were the missionary workers who went South to enlighten the freedmen after the results of that conflict had given the Negroes a new status. These earnest workers, however, had more enthusiasm than knowledge. They did not understand the task before them. This undertaking, too, was more of an effort toward social uplift than actual education. Their aim was to transform the Negroes, not to develop them." When mainstream education dictates a certain standard of academic relevance that criteria is followed and deemed certified to educate America's youth. The caveat since the integration of black and white children academically is the mainstream standards set as benchmarks of success for the American student is set with parameters when dealing with black people.

The message to the white liberals that drive into our communities daily to teach black students is that it is now time for you to truly become advocates for supplementing the appropriate educational need for the so-called African Americans. The chapter is entitled, 'Privilege' because to be white in America, one is automatically privy to the constitutional layout of America's promise, "liberty and justice for all." When the constitution was written in 1776 by the founding fathers of this nation, we know as the United States the so-called Negro at the time was enslaved. June 19ᵗʰ, 1865 documents the day in which the so-called Negro was publicized as free of slavery. However, due to the message being slowly conveyed from plantation to plantation, the lack of resources to begin life, to even not being cognizant on how to start this newfound freedom, black people in America during that time were very much still psychologically enslaved. The philosophies of Marcus Garvey,

Cedric A. Washington

Booker T. Washington, and W.E.B. Du Bois inspired and motivated Negroes across America to go back to Africa, pull yourself up by your bootstraps and show your worth, as well as be educated because if black people are to be free it's up to black people to teach and cultivate them to reach those heights.

America, built off the blood, sweat, tears, and equity of the enslavement of Hebrew Israelites (Deuteronomy Chapter 28) created the social norms, policies, and procedures of how people are to flourish in the land of the free, home of the brave. This blueprint established propaganda which created superiority of white people and the inferiority of black people. Systems that were engraved into play found a poetic way of painting the imagery of hatred towards black people by white people and embedded a certain level of contempt within black people in America. From the economy to education to community living a systematic structure laid the foundation to keep the so-called African American advancing no higher than the figurative glass ceiling of success. The history, culture, language, beliefs of the so-called Negro in America was dissipated through slavery. To practice any cultural idiosyncrasies during the time of slavery by black people were threatened and abused by their oppressor, thus discouraging the so-called Negroes to exist organically within themselves in their culture but take on a tumultuous lifestyle of being a second-class citizen in foreign land to them. This predicate as to why the white liberal teacher in urban education should understand the miseducation of the so-called negro, so-called black people, and/or so-called African American. We have been stripped of our natural culture and origin while having to download and learn a jaded perspective of historical American

History, poor schooling choices due to housing segregation, wealth disparities and are educated through a system that does not provide the so-called African American with a stable sense of knowledge of self.

To the white liberal teacher that teaches urban education in America your voice is needed just as much as the African Americans that speak to the ills of society. We need you to allocate resources and explain to the policy creators that there is no way an individual can be properly educated to advocate for himself or herself without the proper information and people teaching them. For slavery to be such a cornerstone of American History there must be a required class for all to have African American Studies. Without the adequate teaching of the whole spectrum there will always be a disproportionality of learning when it comes to the so-called African American because of the isolated instances of history that are taught in traditional charter, public and private schools. Education is not an occupation; It is an opportunity to provide insight to individuals to enhance their academic, social, emotional, mental, physical wellbeing. In hopes to equip people with the necessary knowledge to become outstanding civilians to teach others, to exist and live in harmony. When you look at the inner cities across America, the educational system, the economy, housing, and neighborhoods in comparison to suburban areas there is a clear disproportion. If you are a white liberal teacher teaching in a black school, in a black neighborhood, educating black kids and you live in a different area than your job then you see the clear difference. It is not noble of you to emphatically be enthusiastic about working in a black school because

Cedric A. Washington

you're thinking you are helping or giving back when the system is still being perpetuated to our demise. It is time to help scrap the system of miseducation and create a system of empowering the African American community to withstand independence of themselves. To be quiet currently, to step aside currently, to think I teach black kids, love the black culture, it's not me it's the past is not enough. To change the behavior of black children that we see today, we must change our intelligence. Intelligence is provided through culture. Everything cannot always be taught by manual. Often, then not, the intelligence of an individual comes from rearing. Rearing is cultural. If you consider yourselves an ally to the black community then you are understanding for a community to truly evolve, we must be led by us. We must be taught by us. Those that do not know their history are bound to repeat it.

The MISEDUCATION OF THE NEGRO

IN THE 21st CENTURY

Chapter 2

Figurehead.

"I don't always agree with the rules, but this is what they want us to do.," "Sometimes you gotta play the game, man.," "This is this man's business, and he wants to run things the way he wants it done." I call these figurehead-isms. From the Definitions of Oxford Languages, figurehead is defined as, a nominal leader or head without real power. That is the majority of the black principals in America. In 1933, Woodson said, "the Negro's mind has been all but perfectly enslaved in that he has been trained to think what is desired of him. The "highly educated" Negroes do not like to hear anything uttered against this procedure because they make their living in this way, and they feel that they must defend the system. Few mis-educated Negroes ever act otherwise; and, if they so express themselves, they are easily crushed by the large majority to the contrary so that the procession may move on without interruption."

Reading that passage for the first time and reflecting on my experiences with black principals I was astonished how relevant that passage was in the 21st Century. Black principals in education are the epitome of being in between a rock and a hard place. It is admirable for a teacher to progress through the ranks of education. For those that took the administrative challenge to lead a school in any capacity has always had my utmost profound respect. Taking a vision of a school and implementing best practices to guide a staff to increase test scores, improve attendance,

Cedric A. Washington

curtail behavior and discipline, engage parents, and most importantly educate kids is a daunting task that is not to be taken lightly. However, the miseducation of black students in America appears to be accepted by the black leaders of schools. And, not just the principals, but also by the board members. Leadership turns into a badge of honor and a level in which those that aspire and are ambitious enough to embark towards the top find themselves in the grand scheme of things just the face of the business.

At the top is even more scarce when it comes to black people being in charge. The badge of honor for being accepted to play a leadership role for black people becomes the muzzle put over their mouth. Rising to the top, translates to shaking and nodding your head. The policies and decisions that are put in place by the authorities are instructed to the black principal for implementation to the school. A principal's worst nightmare is dysfunctionality. Dysfunctionality, particularly in the eyes of their boss. So, to secure their respective position the black principals proceed to exploit black children in the worst way academically. "Sweat the small stuff" is a phrase that is casually used when describing how to create strong discipline within a school's culture. The idea is to start off the school year intensified. And, for every concrete jungle in America the school to prison pipeline production begins its course.

School to prison pipeline has been a controversial topic for the last 20-25 years in educational circles. According to researchers that present on the topic, school to prison pipeline is a term of policies and practices that pushes students out of the classroom into the criminal justice system which mainly affects children of color What Educators Can Do to Help Dismantle the School-to-Prison Pipeline | NEA. From entering the building through metal detectors, strict uniform and id policy, silent lunches, zero- tolerance criteria regarding behavior and discipline for students, suspensions, and expulsions a large majority of schools have adopted these methods which finds black schools and black students in predominantly white schools receiving the brunt of these disciplinary actions. Tyrannical policies and practices coupled with the presence of law enforcement in the schools all creates this educational discord that adheres to the miseducation of the Negro in the 21st Century. And all while simultaneously creating a school culture to have well behaved children or the attempt to be incident free during a school day, teachers are in the classrooms teaching a mainstream curriculum that reflects truly little of the population they are serving. The black principal under the doctrine of being a miseducated negro themselves is showing no more of an understanding of the objective before us than the white liberal teacher who comes in naively with the intent to teach our youth. Yet, the job security and probability of being a successful leader is the motivation for the black principal. Unfortunately, to find them all in the Hunger Games of who's who of running the next miseducated institution of the Negro, black people, or African American students.

To the black principal it is imperative for you to acknowledge the theory of the miseducation of the Negro. Since desegregation, and the execution of integrating black people and white people academically and economically, the so-called African Americans education and business dissolved in the concept of the American way. Black people's perspective has always been an afterthought in the

Cedric A. Washington

big picture. To continue to perpetuate a system that is ill-suited for black students has ended. There are too many resources, research, and intelligence to continue to go down a pathway of destruction. To the black principal to be a figurehead in your position in the 21st century is no different than the 'house negro' analogy in Malcom X's speech, 'The House Negro vs. Field Negro'. The black people of America have been stripped of their natural origin to be enslaved in America. The miseducation of the Negro in the 21st Century must be derailed by your efforts to bring light to this matter. To build up children, one must teach the children; If it takes a village to raise a child then it's up to the village to teach their culture. A village will never thrive with the miseducation of their people, who grow up to become misinformed adults. Misinformed adults raise misinformed children to create a misinformed society and that is the recipe for chaos and confusion. To the black principal, you cannot create a conducive school culture for black children to learn and it's void of their culture. To be proud of self, to have knowledge of self, one must learn self. To the black principal, we need your conscience awakened to lead our youth to the proper path of learning true intelligence. If we are not actively building up ourselves and our communities through true knowledge, then we will find ourselves on the everlasting hamster wheel of learning and the figurative glass ceiling of success in America.

The Miseducation of the Negro
in the 21ˢᵗ Century
Chapter 3
Knowledge vs. Education.

Knowledge is defined as facts, information, and skills acquired by a person through experience or education, the theoretical or practical understanding of a subject. Education is defined as the process of receiving or giving systematic instruction, especially at a school or university (Oxford Languages). For clarity, I like to define terms, so people can comprehend the content at hand. The words knowledge and education, although synonyms, shows the distinct difference of how through one aspect you are systematically taught to learn. If your oppressor controls your academic intelligence, then you are bound to only learn what they desire you to know; that can result in a miseducation.

To delve into this matter more intently I want to discuss the Collaborative Academic Social Emotional Learning model known as CASEL. SEL (Social Emotional Learning), in short, consists of five core competencies: Self Awareness, Self-Managing, Social Awareness, Relationship skills, and Responsible decision making 15 Activities for Teaching CASEL Core Competencies - Waterford.org . The objective of this nationwide initiative amongst schools and after school settings in SEL (Social Emotional Learning) is to converge academics and behavior to meet the needs of students in hopes to prepare a healthy balance of social/emotional awareness to get students to perform adequately in school. Again, the caveat to such a

Cedric A. Washington

deed is the one size fits all approach when it comes to education.

Self-Awareness is the first unit of SEL (Social Emotional Learning). In my research, studying social emotional learning I came to the realization of how shallow the concept is when dealing with the so-called African American youth. The American Academy of Family Physicians states, "self-awareness strengthens one's resilience by allowing one to be aware of internal cues, be insightful on one's own strengths and weakness, and understands blind spots and lenses." In this finding, I have concluded that identity has escaped from this important feature in self-awareness. How can one truly have self-awareness if you do not have proper identity? Identity is the distinguishing character of personality or an individual; the relation established by psychological identification (Merriam Webster). Under the premise of mainstream education, students are compacted in with the concept of over generalizing children in a certain stage of adolescence as if culture does not placate certain behavior or intelligence. Thus, inadequately being able to shape the so called African American student appropriately because mainstream curriculums miss the mark on the specific audience that struggles the most socially and emotionally, the miseducated negro. Upon interaction in any capacity of greeting a person the first thing you are introduced to is their identity; you notice one's gender, ethnicity/nationality, height, weight, hair texture, etc. And, based on the scenario of interaction the mind automatically goes into an assumption of thoughts based on a person's identity; we speak of this action as a preconceived notion. When the so-called African American student is taught these generic practices, skills, and theories of social emotional learning they are also being taught by people who are jaded themselves by their own ignorance of being improperly educated. In many instances you have the white teacher who has an insufficient understanding regarding the so-called African American culture in which they are charged with the expectancy to provide insight on how the African American students should channel their emotions and thought process. Utterly, finding themselves in the most challenging situation. The education they were provided to be a schoolteacher is now null and void because they can't fathom the cultural characteristics of their students. The lack of cultural connection from teachers, a strict behavior and discipline school policy, and controlled standardized learning are all the elements of the continuation of the miseducation of the Negro in the 21st Century.

As the adage goes, knowledge is power. We discussed in chapter 2 that a miseducation contributes to misinformed parents raising misinformed children that creates a misinformed society and if people are not equipped with the knowledge needed to navigate accordingly, they parish. The duty of imparting knowledge is not solely with the parents; it is a shared action, joint custody, a commitment to advise and counsel the village. The seed of unheard information is the most intricate part of planting knowledge of self within the so called African American people because of cognitive dissonance. The American Psychological Association defines cognitive dissonance as, "an unpleasant psychological state resulting from inconsistency between two or more elements in a cognitive system." Oxford Languages defines cognitive dissonance as

Cedric A. Washington

the state of having <u>inconsistent</u> thoughts, beliefs, or <u>attitudes</u>, especially as relating to behavioral decisions and attitude change. An example of cognitive dissonance is being recognized as black and knowing that our skin is not black. It makes more sense to the eye to be recognized as brown. However, the ideology of being told anything different is quickly to reject the sentiment because of how they were trained to think. Omitting a population of a people's culture and conditioning them to believe an array of ideals leaves the so-called African American skeptical of new information presented regarding knowledge of self.

Knowledge of SELF (Social Empowerment Learning Framework) is a curriculum created specifically for the so-called African American youth and young adults. Through interactive lessons and activities, youth and young adults learn to become self-aware about their identity, gain a thorough understanding of who they are, become socially aware to empower themselves and others, learn to build a society that is beneficial to people in their communities and create short-term and long-term goals to accomplish feats and manage to achieve success. Like the CASEL model, SELF has five mastery steps of knowledge which includes: Self-Conscience, Self-Governing, Social Conscience, Aspirations, and Good People Skills. An example of a lesson/activity in the first unit of Self-Conscience is entitled Love Yourself (The Skin You're In). In this lesson the students are familiarized with the aspects of the term melanin and all the beautiful shades of the so-called African American. Using a skin tone chart, students can align their complexion with the hues of brown on the chart, thus creating critical thinking regarding identifying themselves with a color they are not in black. Discussion is opened regarding the terms black and white and how they are defined. Analyzing the definitions stimulating dialogue on why the so-called African American associates themselves in identifying with a term that has a negative connotation. Especially, when you are taught the power of words and to be intentional with what you say. By the end of the lesson students are empowered and have been educated on the very thing in skin complexion that some so-called African Americans are insecure about today. This is how you cultivate minds through knowledge which produces wisdom to articulate intelligently how they identify themselves. True Knowledge of SELF.

Cedric A. Washington

The Miseducation of the Negro

in the 21st Century

Chapter 4

Culture=Intelligence=Behavior.

"Our experts warned us about the possibility of the phenomenon occurring, for they say the mind has a strong drive to correct and re-correct itself over a period of time, if it can touch substantial original historical base; and they advised us that the best way to deal with the phenomenon is to shave off the brute's mental history and create a multiplicity of phenomena of illusion that each illusion will twirl in its own orbit, something similar to floating balls in a vacuum." Willie Lynch was a diabolical slave owner that addressed the slave owners of the Colony of Virginia in 1712 with the infamous speech, 'The Makings of a Slave'. Admired for his harsh slave tactics in the West Indies he was recommended to speak to the colonizers of Virginia in hopes to facilitate the issues slave owners were experiencing with their slaves. This is important to discuss in correlation with culture, intelligence, and behavior. In some educational circles in the 21st Century the bourgeoisies of the miseducated Negro speaks to the authenticity of the Willie Lynch letter. The audacity of searching for academic credibility regarding the psychological breakdown of our miseducation. As if the content of the theory does not reflect our present-day culture, intelligence, and behavior.

In chapter one, I discussed that rearing was cultural. Culture being the attitudes and behavior characteristic of a particular social group (Oxford Languages). Willie Lynch's speech was to inspire slave owners to create a devilish and dreadful culture for the slaves to behave submissively through near death-like fear. This culture developed an intelligence in the so-called Negroes. Intelligence is defined as a person with the ability to acquire and apply knowledge (Oxford Languages). This slave culture that was created had a plan of division within the enslaved creating a certain intelligence and behavior for the so-called Negroes to survive. Particularly, Willie Lynch emphasized the "nigger female" because she spectated the treatment of the male slaves and already had to deal with the physical and psychological torment of her own. The intent target of the female slave was to ensure that she would rear her children accordingly. Instinctively, she will raise her children with a certain intelligence to behave for survival. Her daughter, she would raise to be independent and negotiable. Her son, in which she would subconsciously fear for his life, she would raise him to be mentally weak and loyal to the slave masters. This cultural rearing dictates the intelligence of the slaves to be submissive and obey their master and if they dare go against the customs of slavery it was hell to pay.

The interloping negative of this deceitful intent to control a group of people came with the warning of familiarity. The purpose was to explain to the slave masters the power of the mind. Intuitively, the mind can correct and re-correct itself over a duration of time if it is sparked by some historical foundation. Being stripped of our culture, native tongue, religious practices, families divided a part all intertwine to help create the miseducation of the Negro (nigger), colored, black, or so-called African/Afro American. This ingenious plan of keeping the miseducated

Cedric A. Washington

Negro depleted of knowledge of self intentionally created a fixed state of extreme fear, unawareness, and depreciation of themselves.

In the modern day, we see the manifestations of this direct trauma. The stigma of the police and the so called African American communities across America share an unhealthy relationship of trust when it comes to protecting and serving the so-called black people. Black people, subconsciously, have passed on from generation to generation a sense of paranoia when it comes to the police. This is attributed due to the disproportionality of injustice when it comes to the so-called African American. Again, you see this in African American mothers when preparing their sons to navigate in the world as teenagers and young adults. They teach their young boys early to always be respectful and govern themselves accordingly in fear that they won't be subjected to a heinous act that we solemnly read about and hear about in outrage every year. In the 21st Century, collectively, black people still identify themselves as a color that they're not. And even more so, categorizing themselves as African American when Africa is a continent that has 534 countries in which a person from that respective country does not identify themselves as African, they associate themselves from which country they are from. Example, a person from Nigeria does not call himself African, they are Nigerians; Ethiopia descent refers to themselves as, Ethiopians, the 44th president of the United States of America, Barack Obama is from Kenya, and he is half Kenyan, etc. If there are 534 countries in the continent of Africa, then what exactly is an African American? There are black people bleaching their skin to be lighter because of the insecurities of being dark, and more than enough black women find themselves discouraged and underappreciated of their natural beauty and hair because of the standard of beauty when it comes to mainstream outlets that dictate what is considered beautiful. This innate intelligence is inadvertently passed down through behavior when a mother is combing her young daughter's hair no older than 5 years old and talks about how "nappy" and "rough" the young girl's hair is and suggests that she needs a perm. When the young girl gets her hair relaxed and it is not as coarse, longer, and a comb can go through smoothly then the young girl is enamored because her mother speaks about how beautiful she looks and how nice her hair is in comparison to before. This type of trained learning perpetuates the type of intelligence and behavior we exude in the present day based on past trauma and depreciation.

A culture is put into place to produce a certain intelligence and behavior. In the 21st Century you can see the disproportion of living when you compare inner cities to suburban areas. The statistics already have proven who predominantly resides in which geographical locations. The culture in the 'hoods' across America has created an unhealthy intelligence that reflects in poor behavioral choices. The environment's lack of resources, run down homes, dilapidated buildings, violence, drugs via drug dealers and users, etc. are characteristics of a negative culture. If one is subjected to this as a normalcy, then how do you expect the intelligence to reflect positive behavior consistently? This outcome is called a product of your environment.

The classic eighties movie Trading Places with Eddie Murphy and Dan Aykroyd was an excellent depiction of this example, intelligence and behavior through

Cedric A. Washington

culture. The gist of the film is centered around natural habits of intelligence and behavior in fixed environments where two savvy brokerage firm owners, who were siblings, made a bet whether it is a person's environment or heredity that determines how one will fare in life. Switching Eddie Murphy, who portrayed a black homeless, conman and Dan Aykroyd, who was a successful white businessman environment and having to adapt to their new environment proved through culture, one will adapt accordingly to survive, as well as take on behaviors that may call for desperate measures or rise to the occasion depending on the resources presented. Intelligence and behavior determined by the elements controlled can produce an outcome of comfort or survival of the fittest. As discussed, the deliberate intent to miseducate a group of people to control their minds has propelled generations of passed down behavior to keep the so-called African American mentally, academically, economically, and socially oppressed. Knowledge is power; the mind can correct its thought process once it is familiarized through some identification of its natural origin. For that to happen we must control our destiny; our intelligence and behavior is solely contingent upon that.

The Miseducation of the Negro

in the 21st Century

Chapter 5

Parents and the Environment.

Culture=Intelligence=Behavior. Maya Angelou is quoted saying, "When you know better, you do better." But what if you really do not know better? And not because you do not have the mental capacity to comprehend, but because of the environment that molds and shapes your intelligence. Remember, intelligence is the ability to acquire and apply knowledge and skills. The concept of the Willie Lynch theory was to breakdown the slave; keep the body and destroy the mind. In the previous chapter, we discussed how Willie Lynch focused on the "nigger female" and how she watched the treatment of the male slaves in conjunction with her own angst in this created slave culture because she would raise her children to behave in a manner which will keep them compliant with the rules of life for them. The male, the man, is the leader of the family. The man is the protector, the provider for the family. Willie Lynch instructed slave owners to "take the meanest and most restless nigger, strip him of his clothes in front of the remaining male niggers, the female, and the nigger infant, tar and feather him, tie each leg to a different horse faced in opposite directions, set him afire and beat both horses to pull him apart in front of the remaining niggers. The next step is to take a bullwhip and beat the remaining nigger males to the point of death, in front of the female and the infant. Don't kill him, but PUT THE FEAR OF GOD IN HIM, for he can be useful for future breeding." Taking the head of the family, taking the strongest and most

Cedric A. Washington

intimidating of all the men, and torturing him in front of everyone then beating the rest of the men to the point of near death sets the tone for the mentality of the slave, or nigger/negro, colored, black, African/Afro-American man in America.

There is tons of research on the psychological effect of a multitude of scenarios when it comes to the human mind and how people function. On top of respectable scholars researching, documenting, and lecturing particularly, on the demise of the black man in America on a plethora of fronts. So, pick your poison with the angle that you want to indulge in for scholarly rhetoric's sake. There is not a culture in existence in any living form where the male is not the dominant species until you look at the so-called African American man. The so-called African American man is the most disrespected, but most emulated man on the face of the earth and that is due to the psychological effect of the miseducation of the Negro. One cannot discuss trauma being passed down psychologically and not think that slavery is just as pertinent. The black man in America has always perceived the white man in America having the ability to live freely without feeling controlled or threatened based on their presence. The white man in America has navigated the power of authority when it comes to education, employment, and classism. These three pillars of living find the so-called African American man in an uphill battle of attempting to sustain life for him and his family. Which is why parents, and the environment is crucial for understanding the miseducation of the negro in the 21st Century.

The staggering percentages of the lack of black men heading households of black families across America in the inner cities are mind boggling. What is wrong with the black man in America, that he can't live nobly like his counterparts? It is easier to think that one is full of thoughts of nothingness, excusing the behavior to be upright versus perpetuating the theory of the miseducation of the negro in the 21st Century. Being that it is the 21st Century and although we have progressed through slavery, Jim Crow, Civil Rights era, drug neutralized ghettoes era, Regan, Bush, Clinton, W Bush administrations, first black president era, make America great again era, to an era where we could all witness the slow 8 minutes and forty- six seconds death of a black man at the hands of the police in which put the world into a global frenzy, one would think that the black man in America should by now know to be better, to do better. In every era mentioned it was a demise to the black man, the leader, the head of the family. When the man is removed from the home of a family, statistics show the negative effects of this dynamic despite which nationality you originate from. The black man in America disproportionally has higher rates of absenteeism in the homes which results in behavior of the children, negatively. This disproportionality effects the black community in an abundance of ways: lack of positive black male role models (which is why the high demand for mentoring), lack of representation of how to be a husband or father or how to treat a husband or father (the latter is rarely discussed in the black community), to even the lack of ability to work together as black men, collectively. These dynamics are just a few of the orbital balls in a vacuum that the Willie Lynch theory spoke of when explaining how this trained conditioning will manifest itself in other ways throughout the generations of time. And we see it in real time because it is documented and researched, year in and out.

Cedric A. Washington

Misinformed adults raising misinformed children to create a misinformed society due to a miseducation of people describes the black parents and black environment in the 21st Century. Parents are not participating in their children's education proactively in many of the black communities across America. Blindly, black parents believe in and allow implementations of the schools to enrich their children through academics and social teaching because they do not know any better themselves. The vulgarity of talk by black students towards adults, the blatant disrespect of teachers by black students, the other half of the reason the school to prison pipeline exists is because of the behavior of black students. This atrocity of behavior from students in the inner cities of urban education comes directly from the teachings of the parents and the environment. Often parents are not surprised by their child's behavior because their response is, "that's how they are at home." The black family in many ways have spiraled out of control and just as the black family has dispersed, so has the accountability of our environment.

There was a time in which black people were respectful about the community. A community of people in a black neighborhood during the sixties, seventies, and even the early eighties came with an unspoken rule of accountability. The black community parented each other's children for the sake of instilling manners, respect, and hospitality amongst each other. During these times, the black father was relevant in the homes of the black family. In the 21st Century the audacity of redirecting a child's behavior; you might get reprimanded by the child and followed up by a verbal lashing of the parent. Some parents are delusional when it comes to admitting the shortcomings of behavior for their own children. Thus, not seeking the appropriate guidance to ensure their child is being properly addressed. This created environment (culture) of the 'hood' breeds a mentality (intelligence) that ignites through actions (behavior) which causes a code of ethics living in the 'hood.'

We see it in a lot of ways in this type of environment, one being black students' reluctance to show they are smart. Not wanting to volunteer to answer questions, deliberately answering a question with the wrong answer to be funny, or even lashing out in a defense mechanism because they do not want to speak in front of the class are all behaviors shown amongst black students more often than one would like. This is the environment that is being created amongst black students in schools atop of an already biased mainstream curriculum and being forced to learn an inadequate part of history and merely nothing pertaining to themselves, lack of cultural competent teachers, law enforcement in the school building, a strict uniform and id policy, zero tolerance behavior and discipline policy, suspensions, and expulsions without any real intervention on how to fix the black community and the people in it. If we want change to occur amongst our people, we must first be able to collectively organize. There are too many orbital balls floating around (agendas) that take the black community off focus. Everyone has a plight and wants their plight to be addressed without realizing that the common denominator for every plight is being black. The black woman is the most unprotected and the black man is the most disrespected person in America. Until we realize that we need each other to save our environments then we will continue to be submerged in unintelligence and idiotic behavior

Cedric A. Washington

because we are producing children that are born into a society that hasn't a concise direction as to where we are headed as a people.

To the parents and the environment of the miseducated negro in the 21st century it is time to take ownership of your behavior and take control of your communities. The product that is being put out are your children. You cannot expect an oppressor that has set the benchmark of success regarding how far they would allow you to go to be the same people to help with the dysfunctionality of your neighborhoods. That is the plan for controlling the slave. If the powers that be are continuing to manipulate our environment by controlling the elements and we don't step up to take over our own, then we will continue to matriculate down the path of destruction of our environments, inevitably.

The Miseducation of the Negro

In the 21st Century

Chapter 6

Hip-Hop.

Since 2017, Hip-Hop has been the number 1 music genre in the world according to Billboard. Not too bad for some "rap mess" as the older people would say when I was a child growing up in Gary, Indiana. The year was 1973 in the boogie down Bronx, NY where the culture was created that would give myself and a host of others in inner cities across America the style and grace to walk, talk, dress, dance, rap, beatbox, expressing ourselves through art and music in which ultimately would be shared by the world. Chuck D, of Public Enemy, coined Hip-Hop as the black CNN giving an insight to white America regarding the struggles and disproportionalities of the ghettos across the U.S.A. The legendary rap group N.W.A. (Niggaz with Attitudez) provided the perspective of oppressed frustration with the injustices of law enforcement in Compton, CA in which other urban cities across the nation could relate to as people chanted at concerts, rhymed with the lyrics word for word in their cars, as well as watched the video on Yo' MTV raps, 'Fuck Tha Police.' From New York to California and all points in between this phenomenon gave America the audacity to go into an ethical hysteria because just like the neutralized drug war spilled over from the hood to the suburbs, hip-hop began to do the same. The Hip-Hop culture spread like a germ, infectiously taking a mainstream turn to marketing commercials, being paired with sports figures, to glorifying the ghetto's most notorious lifestyle in the drug game. The hobby that most

Cedric A. Washington

thought would only be a phase aggressively transformed into one of the most controversial, yet popular genres known to the music industry.

The egregious stories that have been shared by innumerable artists of all types regarding the business of the music industry has given us insight on how artists can either be successful financially or fail depending on contracts and how detailed you are in understanding the business. This is imperative in mentioning because of the premise of the music business structure. Record companies draw up contractual agreements to recording artists to create their music. And what is peculiar about the jargon of the contracts, preferably are the usage of the term's "master" and "slave" in reference to the recordings of the music. The exploitation of black artists in which fathered a lot of the genre styles we know and love today in Rock & Roll, Pop, Blues, Country, R&B and Hip-Hop find themselves perplexed as to how they aren't the masters, which means they are the owners of their intellectual property. And the slaves are the copies of the recording that are produced from the machine that makes the original recording.

"Master and slave are terms that have long been commonly linked to indicate a dominant/subservient relationship in electrical engineering and in many a recording studio. In the pre-digital era, in the context of recorded music, the terminology referred to the duplication process; it was a way of distinguishing between source recordings and the physical copies that were pressed from them and distributed for retail sale. Columbia, the oldest label in America, was founded in 1889 and credited with the "invention of the flat disc record," per the company's own boilerplate" (Halperin and Helligar).

"The history of enslavement has always haunted the music industry and always structured it," says Josh Kun, chair in cross-cultural communication at USC Annenberg School for Communication and Journalism. "If you go back to the first Black artist to ever make a commercial musical recording in the 1890s George W. Johnson, was a former slave who began his life not owning his own body, being owned by a master, then [went on] to record a master that he did not own. This also gets at the long-standing belief and conviction of so many Black artists, throughout the 20th century and into this one, that they have been treated like slaves by the masters who they signed contracts with. That's been true since the early 1900s, and it is certainly true now." How Pharrell Williams Is Breaking the Chains of Music's Troubled Past - Variety So, Hip-Hop is the number one music genre in the world. And, learning the basis of the music business one can take away that the formation of its structure resembles slavery and not just because of the chosen terminology, but also due to the unjust treatment of owning intellectual property and profiting from it. Which brings me back to 'The House Negro vs. Field Negro' speech in comparison to the miseducation of the negro in the 21st Century, Hip-Hop and the music business. Malcolm X explained that the two types of slaves differed in ways; one being the house negro was obedient to the slave master. And the field negro despised the slave master and wanted to devise a plan to escape any way possible at any given time. During this slave culture, the house negro was the confidant to the slave master. The house negro, traditionally, was positioned to keep an eye out for the master to ensure that the field negroes were complying. In many instances, the house negro also was granted the

Cedric A. Washington

authority to whip some of the slaves. This continued to drive a division in between the community of the enslaved. Privilege strategically was sanctioned to a chosen few while the masses were subjected to hell on earth. However, in its moment of clarity the house negro too was reminded that they were merely servants to this devilish cause.

Culture=Intelligence=Behavior. Hip-Hop is an African American culture. It is our duty as a people to protect it. The miseducation of the negro in the 21st Century is impacted by the negative effects of some rap music. Music is a mood setter. As a former college basketball player, I would listen to certain joints (songs) to get my adrenaline rushing before a game. When I am with my lady, and I want to set a romantic ambiance then my playlist will consist of songs that will set the mood for that moment. My critical thinking question to you is if the majority of the inner cities across America are plagued with violence, drugs, sexual promiscuity, blatant disrespect amongst each other in various capacities do you think that a certain type of music could be an element to help perpetuate this behavior?

To the rappers of the hip hop community, particularly those that are considered 'Gangsta Rappers' we need you too, conscience to understand the miseducation of the negro in the 21st Century. I am old enough to have witnessed gangster rap growing from being an unheard perspective of what is going on in the black communities to being a glorified perspective that people want to emulate for clout. The "Wanksta" that 50 Cent spoke of is due to the parents and the environment talked about in the previous chapter. The Black man, the head, the lead, the protector of the people's mind has been warped through a miseducation. We live in a time where we consider each other "ops" while simultaneously, living in a world of proposed inequality from our oppressor. We cannot afford you to perpetuate that character any longer. The existence of the future of our people depends on your conscience and the type of music you make. The rap game is the only genre of music I know that the lines of art imitating life and life imitating art are blurred. The bravado and machismo that is coupled with rappers that cause public beefs that has led to deaths only happens in Hip-Hop. Again, what is wrong with the black man in America that he can't live nobly like his counterparts? The privilege of being able to display your talent to the world, travel, live exceptionally well, not having to struggle like the people in communities that patronizes and emulates your music to help cause our demise is equivalent to the characteristics of the House Negro. You move out of the hood and go live in a better environment all while creating music that does not reflect the new lifestyle that you are currently living. And this music is listened to and inspired by so many youth that have not a clear direction of heading down the right path because of the lack of positive black male role models in the hood amongst all the other negative elements of the environment. We need your conscience to understand that Hip-Hop was created to tell a story not sell a story. And when you allow people to dictate your intellectual property for financial gain to portray a certain image through a type of music, you are selling your people out to the cause.

The field negro was the masses. There were always more of the field negroes than the house negroes. Hip-Hop is our culture. There are more teachers in our culture than there are rappers in the limelight. It is my duty as a teacher of the people to help cultivate

Cedric A. Washington

the hip hop culture. That duty is not solely for rappers just as the duty to impart knowledge and wisdom is not solely on the parents to teach their children; that's why we have school. If it takes a village to raise the child, then understand the hip hop community has more than just the voice of the rappers to speak on our culture. It is important to control the narrative of our culture to avoid the continuation of the miseducation of the negro in the 21st Century.

Music, sports, entertainment brings a community of people together no matter the gender, nationality, or culture. The Hip-Hop community in many ways has desensitized the word nigger (nigga) through rap music. Obviously, being now the number 1 music genre in the world, hip hop is enjoyed by all. Rap lyrics are sung in unison at concerts in which the unspoken rule of not saying the word by white people are usually respected, but the younger black generation in some settings has appeared to allow the word to be a term of endearment that can be affectionately shared by their white friends. In the 21st Century few of us comprehend that the word used to describe us because of our skin complexion originates from the Latin word 'Niger' (ny-jer) meaning black which through Spanish and Portuguese people pronounce and spell it 'Negro' (Oxford Languages). Negro is a color not a nationality or origin. Christopher Columbus completed four Spanish based voyages in which he described the darker complected people he encountered and colonized in Africa as 'Negro.' Nigger is a created term in annunciation and pronunciation by white people that spoke of other dialects that colonized themselves in America as our ancestors were enslaved; a term that was intently used to demean us. The miseducation of the so called

African American in America has us defining the term nigger (nigga) differently depending on annunciation and connotation. In chapter three, I discussed cognitive dissonance being the key factor in teaching knowledge of self to the so-called black people in America. We are not negroes, niggers, colored people, or black people; these titles all indicate a specific color, black. Every other human being, even Caucasian (white) people can pinpoint a place of origin for their ancestry. The so-called African American is just a culmination of Africa and America not specifying a distinct nationality of people. To the Hip-Hop culture the time has come for our people to be conscious of who we are and take control of our destiny. The miseducation of the negro in the 21st Century desperately needs your conscience and your voice. Wake yo' ass up!

Cedric A. Washington

The Miseducation of the Negro

In the 21st Century

Chapter 7

Politics.

"I pledge allegiance to the flag of the United States of America, and to the republic for which it stands, one nation under God, indivisible, with liberty and justice for all." The Pledge of Allegiance was originally written in August 1892 by socialist minister Francis Bellamy The Pledge of Allegiance (ushistory.org). Dates interest me in history regarding America because I find myself aligning the so-called African American people with our status in the land of the free when these proclamations are declared. Jim Crow laws, in which Jim Crow was named after a black minstrel show character lasted from 1865 the end of the Civil War through 1968. This is essential in discussion because for 103 years on American soil it was blatant legalized racial segregation that prevented us the right to vote, maintain employment, get an education amongst a list of other things and this is after 246 years of chattel slavery. In 1965 under President Lyndon B. Johnson the so-called black people in America were finally given the liberty and justice of the right to vote after numerous diabolical attempts to keep colored people from experiencing democratic freedom this one nation under God provides for the people. The irony of it all is a Republican (Right Wing) party president in Abraham Lincoln "freed" the slaves in America and a Democratic (Left Wing) party president in Lyndon Johnson passed the voting act for the so-called negro to vote in America. But the injustices and disproportionalities of living still haunted and haunts the so-called black people of America despite which wing of the American eagle (United States seal) dictates the so-called black people of America's destiny. Opportunities, employment, and justice has been an on-going theme for the so-called negro, colored, black, or African American in the United States of America and to the republic for which it stands. Negro, colored, black, African American, I use these titles frequently because each title represents a phase in American history that describes the descendants of the people of ancient Israel (Deuteronomy 28) that were brought over involuntarily from northern Africa across the Atlantic Ocean to build up the Americas. To put our latest term of classification, African American in perspective, January 31st, 1989 The New York Times front page read an article titled, "African-American Favored by Many of America's Blacks" which showed you that the term African American is yet another created way to describe the so-called black people in America. African American was used in scholarly circles in the eighties but gained its notoriety during the 1988 presidential campaign of Reverend Jesse Jackson Jr. The 1990 Census Bureau didn't have time to change the classification before going out to the public, so the box African Americans checked read Negro/Black to be counted as a citizen in the U.S. of A 'African-American' Favored By Many of America's Blacks - The New York Times (nytimes.com).

The miseducation of the negro in the 21st Century finds black people still proclaiming they are Democrats or Republicans. The miseducation of the negro in the 21st Century finds the so called African American STILL asking for opportunities, employment, and justice. Hip-Hop discussed in chapter 6 is the most popular music genre in the

Cedric A. Washington

world and during the campaign of what would be the 44th president of the U.S.A. hip-hop helped Senator Barack Obama in a major way ushering in African Americans to vote with the slogan "Vote or Die" through record setting numbers for our communities. Only to STILL have niggas asking for a black agenda after having President Barack Obama, the first "black" president in office for 8 years (2008-2016). The Black Greek Letter organizations catapulted the Democrat Party again in 2020 backing what would be the nation's first woman and black Vice President, Kamala Harris in the White House with their "Pearls and Chucks" initiative solidifying, a victory for current president (46th) Joe Biden. Only to STILL ask for opportunities, employment, and justice.

To the so-called black people of America, it is time for you to understand the power, influence, and most importantly who you truly are to debunk the miseducation of the negro in the 21st Century. It is time for us to come together collectively to fulfill the black agenda. We rally together at times, and it is magical. In 2018, you could not tell a black person in America they weren't from Wakanda. The royalty, the majestic, the militant, the unity, the beautifulness we embodied during that period proved how dope of a culture we look together. We are beautiful people of all hues of brown that do not mind boasting off its swag and beauty. And, as capturing as that moment in time was, it was only a mere fiction of entertainment for us.

It is time for us to be that assertive collectively in advocating for our communities. We own absolutely anything that we patronize in our communities that can matriculate dollars for us to stay in our respected environments to thrive efficiently. Koreans, Arabs, Indian Americans have seemed to cut the line in climbing the ladder to success. We are taking the stairs and they are climbing escalator style. No Democrat or Republican can help us with that. That is something the people must organize and construct on our own if we want to fix our problems. But we are preoccupied with the hamster wheel of life that is perpetuating the system because of the gamble of not being able to survive adequately. The needle is moved where we have successfully gained middle class status for some, and the problems become social-economic status issues versus Black people issues. Meanwhile, the rich get richer, and another four years would have gone past, and we will be in search of STILL for a black agenda because we need opportunities, employment, and justice.

Collectively, on any given level of the socio-economic class (upper, middle, and lower) the so-called Black people in America are always reminded of that figurative glass ceiling. The power that black athletes have in the NBA and NFL is insurmountable. You can never be replaced. We need you too conscience of the miseducation of the negro in the 21st Century. Your voice and platform are very much needed. If America can send her best talent to participate in world games to boast its GOD given ability athletes to win Gold, then for sure she can repay her appreciation of dominance by taking care of her own. Combining the sources of our people through the athletic and entertainment industry is enough to start the process of a Black Wall Street in every region of America, east coast, mid-west, down south, and west coast. The late Paul Mooney articulated best, "everybody wanna be a nigga, but don't wanna be a nigga." The impact and influence we have, once we start helping ourselves there are a world of others that

Cedric A. Washington

are willing to facilitate the cause. GOD helps those that help themselves. To my people in the inner cities that are tired of the flaws of the system, the time is now to begin to help yourself. The power of the black dollar can manifest everything and more that we need to create a culture to produce positive intelligence and exemplary behavior. Helping ourselves means we are making the world a better place. Then the negative stereotypes and myths that are often shared can begin to turn into the brilliance and boldness of the many powerful people that need to be cultivated and given a chance through their own. Advocating as a party for us, the so-called African Americans does not mean we are anti any nationality, religion, organization or encouraging hate towards any people. That narrative is asinine as if cultures cannot exist without ill intent. We demand true freedom, justice, and equality. "No civilization is conquered from outside until it destroys itself from within." The time is now to destroy the miseducation of the negro in the 21st Century and build who we are chosen to be. Fin.

The Miseducation of the Negro

In the 21st Century

Chapter 8

The Black Church.

Keep the body and destroy the mind! And if this grueling process is done properly, it will refuel itself innately over time. He spoke of various orbits spinning on its axis, meaning the culture created will develop a multitude of issues psychologically and socially such as distrust, fear, adulation, depreciation, inferiority, to name a few. These characteristics are shown as cognitive dissonance in people. The so-called black people of America have been told so little about their lineage and have been brainwashed into believing various concepts regarding knowledge of themselves that it's hard to convince them of the truth. Now couple this tactic with the ultimate manipulation in governing your religious beliefs and you have mastered how to control a group of people successfully. The miseducation of the negro in the 21st Century has black people believing in the same religion as their oppressor. The ultimate manipulation of controlling a group of people is through their worship and spiritual beliefs. Praying for a better day without working towards the better day seems to be the disconnect of teaching in the black church. We can experience blatant racism in the world, but rarely is it discussed in the church for understanding how to navigate as a people in the 21st Century. That message is evaded and vaguely put to call on Jesus. The black church doesn't distinguish the fact of two totally separate descriptions given towards Jesus that we're told to call on. Sadly, it is the most dismissive sentiment regarding the Christianity belief. Most

Cedric A. Washington

miseducated negroes of the 21st Century love to say, "I don't care what color he is. All I know is that he died for my sins." That is a miseducation. Everything has definitive answers except religion. That is when it is up to the interpretation, hence the many denominations of Christianity.

Slavery happened. Then Jim Crow happened. Which led us to the Civil Rights Movement because we wanted to be treated equally. Then here we are decades later post George Floyd, yet Christianity is the religion of choice for America; the oppressor and the oppressed are considered Christians. The moral of the bible is the battle of good versus evil; right versus wrong. What is left up to the interpretation is who is on which side of the coin. What are we being taught as the so-called negro, colored, black, or African American to understand this psychological and spiritual warfare in church? Since 1968 black people in America have had the luxury to participate in having civil rights. That is a total of 55 years to put that in perspective. How can a nation of people because there are forty-one million of us (black people) in America gain traction to an equal playing field in such a brief time under so many restrictions? That must have some sort of moral compass on it for this one nation, under God, indivisible with liberty and justice for all. What are we doing black church? Or do we call on Jesus? The black church in the 21st Century is entertainment. It is a feel-good message with no real sustenance to guide us collectively as a people. Everybody is lumped in as GOD's children. Then why was such a devilish plan put in place to enslave a group of people if we are all GOD's children. The miseducation of the negro in the 21st Century will have you leaning over to your neighbor and saying, "Favor ain't fair." All while demanding 55 years later after the Civil Rights Movement, opportunities, employment, and justice. Because it must be some sort of favor for white people to live disproportionally better than black people. Christianity was strategically used to control slaves in America. The buy-in were the slave preachers whose duty was to go around to the plantations to preach the gospel. Ephesians 6:5-6 is a scripture that was the foundation of manipulating the slaves to believe that obeying their earthly masters, the nice ones and the harsh ones was pivotal regarding them going to heaven. When history is sparsely mentioned and vaguely put it is difficult to fathom a time without thoroughly explaining the moment. Let me remind you that our ancestors were in foreign land to them, had to learn a new language, and practice a religion that was also practiced by the people who enslaved them. And, most notably it was illegal for the so-called Negro in America to read or write.

Nat Turner, who is famously known for one of the bloodiest slave Revolts in Southampton County, Virginia understood for every scripture in the bible that was used to condemn it was a scripture used to uplift. And that is where the attempt to control became a problem because Nat Turner began to have knowledge. The knowledge developed into wisdom which gave him the courage to rebel against the education that he was instructed to give the slaves on the plantations through this Christianity religion. He was hanged in celebratory fashion in front of the whole town, the white people, and the black slaves for causing an uprising in an attempt to set his people free of bondage. However, depending on which side

Cedric A. Washington

of the coin you are viewing, this is a heroic effort or terrorism.

Nobel Peace Prize Winner, the good Reverend Dr. Martin Luther King Jr. whom in which is internationally known for his church background and most importantly the "turn the other cheek" approach of gaining equality that spearheaded the Civil Rights Movement was assassinated in his efforts for causing an uprising in attempt to set his people free of bondage. Dr. King was very intentional in suggesting if you cannot be nonviolent do not get involved, and ironically died violently, admittedly years later at the hands of the government.

The Honorable Elijah Muhammad under the teachings of Master Fard Muhammad led great masses of black men and women into the teachings of Islam. Taking a turn from the traditional teachings of America's religion, Mr. Muhammad emphasized for black people to gain freedom, justice, and equality through unification of black people solely. Through his guidance and teaching revered master teachers like Malcolm X and Louis Farrakhan that continued to spread the gospel of knowledge and unity for the so-called black people in America. Yet, through its empowering messages to the African American people the Nation of Islam only created a division of black people in churches on a Sunday with the majority of black Americans choosing to be Christians. Not to mention in the height of the Civil Rights Movement it was a democratic selection amongst who would be the chosen leader for our people with some siding with the philosophies of Malcolm X and those that chose to follow Dr. King's theory. Which manifested another orbital ball (agenda) in which faith-based path to take as a black person in America. The CIA and the FBI has always been linked to the great leaders of the so-called negro, colored, black, or African American people. COINTELPRO documented the so-called negro leaders every move with informants and constant observations of every action. With turmoil within the Nation of Islam and a disharmony of beliefs and actions, Malcom X found himself clashing with the very person he credited his awakened conscience in Elijah Muhammad. Malcolm X was assassinated on a Sunday afternoon in front of a congregation of people that included his wife and three young daughters.

Slave revolts to gain freedom, justice, and equality. A civil rights movement to gain freedom, justice, and equality. Nonviolent approach to gain freedom, justice, and equality. By any means necessary approach to gain freedom, justice, and equality. A Christian approach to gain freedom, justice, and equality. An Islamic approach to gain freedom, justice, and equality. Every aspect of attempting to gain freedom, justice, and equality in this one nation, under GOD, indivisible with liberty and justice for all by our people on American ground results in volatile push back from the powers that be in which resulted in death to our leaders. Which contradicts the poetic affirmation of Patrick Henry when he said, "give me liberty or give me death," on March 23rd, 1775, when Mr. Henry was suggesting that it was time to raise militia to the Virginia colony to defend their right to freedom. Warriors like Gideon, Naaman, Samson, King David to name a few are either fictional characters to the black church to inspire how GOD can use you in battle for sermon's sake or these are people that fought for the honor of their people while

Cedric A. Washington

giving GOD the glory for obtaining justice between good and evil.

The miseducation of the negro in the 21st century's biggest culprit is the black church. In the 21st Century you can have a beautiful church with murals of a white Jesus and the twelve disciples throughout the church, a black preacher and congregation members consisting of black people that consider themselves both Democrats and Republicans. The preacher can tell you who to pray to but cannot tell you who to vote for because the Internal Revenue Service (IRS) administers the tax laws written by Congress and has enforcement authority over tax-exempt organizations. What does that all mean? In 1954, Congress approved an amendment by (at the time) Senator Lyndon Johnson to prohibit 501(c) (3) organizations, which includes charities and churches, from engaging in any political campaign activity. To the extent Congress has revisited the ban over the years, it has in fact strengthened the ban. The most recent change came in 1987 when Congress amended the language to clarify that the prohibition also applies to statements opposing candidates Charities, Churches and Politics | Internal Revenue Service (irs.gov). The place of spiritual refuge for people to join corporately, the place where some looked to for answers on how to deal with the injustices of their reality in oppression, the place where the bible is the doctrine that is taught to teach people how to navigate in the world of right and wrong must be selective with discussion when it comes to politics because of government funding. Morally, the church must tread lightly because it is a business. The miseducation of the negro in the 21st Century has created an illusion of thoughts and ideals that has discombobulated the so called African

American to not think intelligently for themselves, but to wait on the Lord. How do you not come together corporately to ensure that your community is choosing the right person to advocate for your neighborhoods? The miseducation of the negro in the 21st Century has dictated an invisible curtain that is pulled down in between one's spiritual belief and political belief as if the two entities are separate in the lives of the so-called African Americans, look at your history. The pastor of a congregation is trusted with the vulnerability of their parishioner's faith when it comes to inspiration, hope, and spiritual guidance. However, cannot speak to the community about who is best suited to lead GOD's people. No different than the separation of church and state when referring to GOD, religion, and the bible in the public schools because it's all left up to an interpretation.

The miseducation of the negro in the 21st Century officially has black people operating within a multitude of balls in a vacuum. The objective was to destroy the mentality of a nation of people to control them. The so-called African American people in America are 41.6 million strong; that is a country of people by itself. That nation of people wept over Trayvon Martin, Jordan Davis, Sandra Bland, Eric Garner, Mike Brown, Philando Castile, Amaud Aubery, Breonna Taylor, George Floyd, and every other black person that has died from the injustices of America through prejudice and racism or died at the hands of black-on-black crime. This curse that GOD put us under that allowed us to be second class citizens in a foreign land to us has given us four hundred years and counting of hell on earth in America the Beautiful. The black church has forgotten that this religion was used to miseducate us. The black church has forgotten that the Ten Commandments were the pillars of living for us, the black church has forgotten that the Genesis of it all started in Israel. Most importantly, outside of the traditional educational system the so-called negro's history dates before slavery and the Atlantic Slave Trade. You can find that information in the Old Testament of the bible; Genesis, Exodus, Leviticus, Numbers, Deuteronomy to name a few. During the Civil Rights Movement, the black church was relevant to community involvement. Now, it is a vague message of individualistic prosperity; every black church is an island on its own with no communal effort to unite with each other for the greater good of the people as a nation. The black church has forgotten that we are the descendants of a nation of people, the tribe of Judah, the children of Israel. The miseducation of the negro in North America was intensified when Willie Lynch lent his theory on how to control a slave. To the nation of the people that was used as production to build up dynasties, railroads, highways, almost any creation in America that you can imagine it is time for us to collectively understand who we are! The revelation is here.

The Miseducation of the Negro

In the 21st Century

Chapter 9

Revelation. (Four hundred Years are Up)

As an educator, being an English Composition, Senior Literature, and African American Studies teacher over the years I've always explained the rule of thumb to my students in using text-based evidence to support your claim/reason/thesis when arguing a point. It's one thing to speak from your opinion which is valid; but the academic world wants you to be professionally researched and read to help solidify your claim made by other people who have researched the topic and most importantly are credited in their efforts. And that's traditionally the first journey to obtaining knowledge vs. education. Research can expound further than the traditional restraints of what mainstream education provides in their curriculum of study. To define miseducation, Merriam-Webster explains it as follows: poor, wrong, or harmful education. Millions of people were uprooted from their original homeland involuntarily in a colonized effort to take over the world. A nation of people were colonized, exiled through trade, murdered and most likely would never see their place of origin again in their natural life. That nation of people are known as the "Children of Israel" or the "Twelve Tribes of Israel." The miseducation comes from who is controlling the narrative to create generations of confused ideologies and thoughts of origin when circumstances begin to develop itself to show and prove these ideals to be false.

Cedric A. Washington

The separation of church and state is the idea that the government should remain neutral toward all religions and not officially recognize or favor any one religion. The problem with this is how we define the usage of the doctrine called the bible. The bible is used in many settings which shows its importance, for example, a person being sworn in as the president of the United States or the bible being used in a court of law as one repeats the oath, "I swear that the evidence that I shall give shall be the truth, the whole truth, and nothing but the truth, so help me God." One book, many denominations converge separately on a Sunday to listen to a preacher speak of a moral lesson which usually concludes on how Jesus is coming to save us all in the end. Yet, the interpretation of the stories of the bible is left up to one's personal denomination. There's the obvious depiction of Jesus Christ that is seen all over the world and then there's Revelation 1:14-15 that reads of subtle differences than what the imagery gives in description of Jesus Christ; his hair on his head white like wool and his feet was like bronze. Then you have the historical aspect of the bible, but school and church are separated, so there's no discussion to elaborate on the history of it. The bible is divided into two testaments, Old and New Testament. According to many modern archaeologists that have researched themselves, the bible is historically accurate even in the smallest of details. The Bible is the holy scripture of the Christian religion, purporting to tell the history of the Earth from its earliest creation to the spread of Christianity in the first century A.D. Noted, both Old Testament and the New Testament have gone through transformations over the centuries which includes the publication of the King James Bible in 1611 and the addition of several books that were discovered later The Bible - HISTORY . The separation of church and state is the gray area of understanding this internationally known doctrine that gives us basic instructions before leaving earth.

Regardless of the educational level, the so-called negro, colored, black or African American's history starts with the Middle Passage, the Transatlantic Slave Trade, and American slavery. Almost magically or instantaneously our history started with trauma which could be the reason it appears that trauma is what sells for black people in America. Just as the stork drops off the baby at the doorstep, America was delivered a nation of people at her doorstep and those people would be used for chattel slavery to build this great nation up to what it is today. Which produces the gray area because the so-called African Americans cognitive dissonance comes into play because pre-slavery history isn't taught in schools. That portion of history is in the Old Testament of the bible that is interpreted by many denominations of Christianity and other religions on Sunday. 'Into Egypt Again with Ships' by Elisha J. Israel is an excellent resource to give a breakdown of our history pre-slavery. I've referenced the book of Deuteronomy chapter 28 periodically because this chapter breaks down the curse that the "Tribe of Judah " will endure after the exodus out of Egypt with Moses when he charged Pharoah to "let my people go". The name Deuteronomy means "second law;" the chapter discusses the Ten Commandments, for a second time in which the Israelites should abide by and if they veered against the word of GOD this time then they will go into Egypt again with ships. Meaning, they would be scattered throughout Africa and abroad, away from their homeland under false religious

Cedric A. Washington

practices, loss of language and culture, tormented and treated unjustly by their captors, etc. As proven in previous chapters we aren't negroes, niggers, colored people, black people or African Americans and this lack of awareness of who we are and being dictated to be named after the slave owners who enslaved our ancestors were a prophesy to what we've experienced and are experiencing in the 21st Century in America.

Politics is a conniving sport that Freudianly doesn't mix with faith because of the underhandedness of exposing their opposing candidates for personal gain. Hence, the reason in 1987 the law was created where no charities or churches (501c3) could speak in opposition of candidates, as well. What sense does it all make? One nation, under God, indivisible with liberty and justice for all, but the deceitfulness of politics to control what is supposedly a democracy shows little faith when it comes to balancing its wings (left and right) for the betterment of the country. President Obama did eight years in office; black people secured the vote. After that, America was made great again for four years for some. Black people in America somberly, were up in arms about a decision and our numbers decreased at the polls. The antics and non-traditional ways of President Donald Trump caused the majority of white America to move hastily and switch gears back to the left wing (Democrats). Again, the black vote helped sway the election because 90% of black women came out to vote for Kamala Harris as the first woman and black Vice President How Black women organized voters to secure Joe Biden's victory (usatoday.com).

The miseducation of the negro in the 21st Century has divided a nation of people in the so-called African

Americans to be pulled in several directions to fulfill agendas of parties that ultimately doesn't have genuine interest in strengthening black America's ability to withstand independence within their own communities. History has shown and proven that no matter the party, Democratic or Republican, the issues of the so-called black people of America remain to be, opportunities, employment, and justice. We are in an era now where the so-called African Americans will unite as one; upper class, middle-class, lower-class levels of black people will begin to work together for the commonality of black people.

America, in the fall of 2019 began to experience an epidemic that wasn't neutralized just for the so-called black people of America. This strand of sickness called COVID-19 took not only the United States, but the world by storm. The world experienced a panic of fear because so many people fell fatally ill, hospitals overcrowded, grocery stores running out of food and toilet tissue, people couldn't leave their homes, children couldn't attend school, parents missing work, creating a pandemic. Literally, four-hundred years later from 1619, in Jamestown, Virginia on August 20th documenting the first arrival of a nation of people scared, separated from families, forced, unwillingly and shackled on ships to America enslaved, the world became uncertain about life. Churches were shut down and couldn't have service and that's when the gray area began to expose the cluelessness of life for billions of people. Nothing made sense. No one knew what to believe. The church was closed. The world sat idled not knowing what was next and that's when EVERYONE saw and felt the kneel that would put America on watch. During a pandemic that was restricted in large public gatherings, billions across

Cedric A. Washington

the world would rally, protest, march, and loot in rage of the continuum of the mistreatment of the so-called African Americans in America. I observed black people praying to GOD to save the country and that's when I realized the miseducation of the negro in the 21st Century would be written.

Revelation is a surprising and previously unknown fact, especially one that is made known in a dramatic way; the divine or supernatural disclosure to humans of something relating to human existence or the world; the last book of the New Testament, recounting a divine revelation of the future to St. John (Oxford Languages). Earlier, I said entertainment brings everyone together, no matter the gender, ethnicity, or class. Opportunity brought everyone to North America in that same fashion; the land is factually known to have an existing civilization. Depending on which side of the coin you're on, one was either brought over unwillingly or you migrated here for a better life. However, the commonality remains that it was someone else's land. Those people are known as the North American Indians (Gad Tribe which is one of the 12 Tribes of Israel). Christopher Columbus and his settlers took over the land and killed over seventy million of the original people and used another twenty million of enslaved Hebrew Israelites to build the land. Every month in October the country showed recognition of this by honoring Columbus Day. Only until recent years is it now recognized in some states as Indigenous People's Day, acknowledged in respect of the North American Indians known as the Gad Tribe.

"...with liberty and justice for all." It's the 21st Century in the year of two-thousand and twenty-three and if humans are honest with themselves, historically or currently there hasn't been a time where it was liberty and justice for all. The gray area of the separation of church and state gives a miseducation to not just the negro in the 21ˢᵗ century, but to all due to various interpretations. Ephesians 6:12 states, "For our struggle is not against flesh and blood, but against the rulers, against the authorities, against the powers of this dark world and the spiritual forces of evil in the heavenly realms" (Bible Gateway). This scripture is very compelling because it explains to us that people aren't naturally hateful, it's the culture that creates an intelligence which develops into a behavior that ultimately becomes your way of life. Again, there's plenty of research to defend this sentiment. Two young toddlers can play with each other innocently, one black and one white without any preconceived notion of the other and develop a genuine embrace of each other. In the same notion a democrat and republican can both root for the same team and have a favorite player that's of a different race than they both are. The genuine adoration for the sport, team, and player is what brings the two together. No ideologies, just the love for a sport. This made-up theory of racism is the established propaganda which created the superiority of white people and the inferiority of black people. There are millions of Caucasian (white) people in the world that aren't racist and are genuinely great people. I'm neighbors with them, I've worked with them, went to college with them, played basketball with them, listened to hip-hop with them, as well as had empowering conversations with them about the world and how the system is designed tougher for us than them. However, these spiritual forces of evil in the heavenly realm are manifested through people; someone must play good, and someone must play evil. The rulers, the

Cedric A. Washington

authorities, and the powers of this dark world control the climate of the game for freedom, justice, and equality. And the separation of church and state is the reason why Jesus will have to come and save us all in the end. There's too many interpretations and one truth. "But about that day or hour no one knows, not even the angels in heaven, nor the Son, but only the Father" (Matthew 24:36). The forever theme of demanding freedom, justice and equality won't ever stop, and the rationing of freedom, justice and equality will always be justified which will keep the so-called African American people always feeling and experiencing civil unrest.

The miseducation of the negro in the 21st Century will begin to be disrupted a lot more unorthodox than its traditional protest. Our minds are beginning to pick up the frequencies of this strong drive to correct and re-correct itself over a period, by being taught properly and recognizing some substantial original historical information. Despite all that the so-called negro, nigger, colored, black, or African Americans has endured over the last four hundred years on American soil we have still persevered to be dominant in what we do. A lot of America's greatest talent, greatest thinkers, greatest orators, greatest inventors, greatest businessmen and women are the so-called African Americans; and that is why we are the chosen people. Marcus Garvey was from the West Indies, he lectured in America to raise funds to help his organization- the Universal Negro Improvement Association of Jamaica. He marveled over the so-called negro in America saying in his speech, 'West Indies in the Mirror of Truth,' "I have traveled a good deal through many countries, and from my observation and study, I unhesitatingly and unreservedly say that the

American Negro is the peer of all Negroes, the most progressive and the foremost unit in the expansive chain of scattered Ethiopia" (Selected Writings and Speeches of Marcus Garvey). Garvey cited a determination of grit and perseverance amongst our ancestors in America. The roses that grew from the concrete jungles around America blossomed into our ancestors' wildest dreams of a better future for those that they left behind. Our duty and due diligence to teach knowledge of self to our people to prevent the continuation of the miseducation of the negro in the 21st Century will be cultivated through learning our culture, implementing our culture, allocating funds through us to help build up our communities and collectively demand of what is owed to us in reparations. Any ally of African Americans by the end of this speech should understand why we deserve reparations; we need your voice too. White liberals in America that inadvertently benefit from the unfairness of the American system your time is here now to walk just as proudly as your ancestors did in the Civil Rights Movement. Hip-Hop is the number one music genre in the world and when rappers look at the sea of crowded people at their concerts, they see the majority of your faces. Support our communities in what really matters, which is our culture, intelligence, and behavior.

To the descendants of the lost Tribe of Judah, who occupy this American land I salute you and your determination to push through. Although the people and our communities have been used as experiments, given inadequate educational opportunities, purposely ran down neighborhoods for planned gentrification, drug infested, lack of employment resources, etc. we still manage to provide for our children, stand in the gap for each other when we needed most, be parents to those that had absent ones, act as coaches, mentors, and teachers to help catapult the great talent, great thinkers, great orators, great inventors, great leaders that we have today; the last shall be first and the first shall be last take your bow, now.

NERD (Nurturing Education Rewarding Determination) Youth Services, Inc. will be a facility in every inner city across America to support our communities in developing our people and not transforming them. Preventative programs to promote mental health and skill development, Knowledge of SELF (Social Empowerment Learning Framework) curriculum to help nurture our youth and young adults holistically in programming will be available daily with interactive lessons and activities through the Project UPLIFT Mentoring program, recreational activities, tutoring for all ages, community room space for baby showers, open houses, conferences, etc., computer labs, basketball courts and swimming pools, arts and craft area, lunch/snacks/dinner provided, and overall safe space for children to share and grow as people in their communities is the vision. My charge to my people is to teach the truth and be a beacon of light to the people as the disciples did for Jesus. GOD sends messengers, prophets, and teachers to teach accordingly. I've learned of my purpose and have figured out my mission for some time now. Throughout my journey I questioned a lot of actions that happened during my career but understood always in the end the greater goal and that was my development to get to this point. I AM a trailblazer. I AM destined to succeed. Speak it. Believe it. Do it.

The Author

Cedric A. Washington is a Published Author, Educational Consultant, International Speaker, TEDx Presenter, and Entrepreneur! Using culturally relevant pedagogical practices to meet state standards teaching English, Composition, Senior Literature, and African American Studies in Gary, Indiana and Chicago, Illinois, Mr. Washington engaged, enlightened, and empowered his students through practical teaching giving his students a sense of knowledge of self. Graduating to the role of administration in education, Washington used a social empowering learning approach advocating for students, mentoring students, and developing young leaders and thinkers to make the right choices and prepare for the next phase of life. The creator of N.E.R.D. (Nurturing Education Rewarding Determination) Youth Services, Inc., Washington is now devoted to teaching and empowering all through his youth services and professional development for educators. Cedric Washington has received numerous accolades for his community service and most notably conducted a workshop for the youth in Washington, D.C. for the Omega Psi Phi Fraternity, Inc. centennial celebration at Howard University. When he is not empowering the people, he enjoys spending time with his family, traveling, listening to music, watching, and playing the game of basketball. His lectures on The Miseducation of the Negro in the 21st Century will inspire educators, leaders, students, and people of the world alike to the truth.

Citation Page.

What Educators Can Do to Help Dismantle the School-to-Prison Pipeline | NEA

15 Activities for Teaching CASEL Core Competencies - Waterford.org

The Willie Lynch Letter and Making of a Slave

Malcom X's Speech House Negro vs. Field Negro

How Pharrell Williams Is Breaking the Chains of Music's Troubled Past - Variety

The Pledge of Allegiance (ushistory.org)

'African-American' Favored By Many of America's Blacks - The New York Times (nytimes.com)

Charities, Churches and Politics | Internal Revenue Service (irs.gov)

The (Scattered) Hebrews: Tribe of Gad | by Black Simba | Medium

The Bible (history.com)

West Indies in the Mirror of Truth, Marcus Garvey

Ghost of Soulja Slim- Jay Electronica ft. Jay-Z

Oxford Languages Dictionary

Merriam Webster Dictionary

Knowledge of S.E.L.F. (Social Empowerment Learning Framework) Curriculum

The Miseducation of the Negro, Carter G. Woodson

APA Dictionary of Psychology

www.ingramcontent.com/pod-product-compliance
Lightning Source LLC
Chambersburg PA
CBHW070030030426
42335CB00017B/2363